UNIVERSITY OF WINCHESTER
LIBRARY

Filter and David Farr

Silence

devised by members of the company

WITHDRAWN FROM
THE LIBRARY
UNIVERSITY OF
WINCHESTER

D1147195

Published by Methuen Drama 2011

Methuen Drama, an imprint of Bloomsbury Publishing Plc

1 3 5 7 9 10 8 6 4 2

Methuen Drama
Bloomsbury Publishing Plc
36 Soho Square
London W1D 3QY
www.methuendrama.com

First published by Methuen Drama in 2011

Copyright © Filter Theatre and David Farr 2011

The authors have asserted their rights under the Copyright, Designs
and Patents Act 1988 to be identified as the authors of this work

ISBN: 978 1 408 15656 8

Available in the USA from Bloomsbury Academic & Professional,
175 Fifth Avenue/3rd Floor, New York, NY 10010.
www.BloomsburyAcademicUSA.com

A CIP catalogue record for this book is available from the British Library

Typeset by Country Setting, Kingsdown, Kent
Printed and bound in Great Britain by
CPI Cox & Wyman, Reading, RG1 8EX

Caution

All rights whatsoever in this play are strictly reserved
and application for performance etc. should be made before
rehearsals begin to Curtis Brown Group Ltd., Haymarket House,
28–29 Haymarket, London SW1Y 4SP. No performance may
be given unless a licence has been obtained.

No rights in incidental music or songs contained in the work are hereby granted
and performance rights for any performance/presentation whatsoever must be
obtained from the respective copyright owners.

No part of this publication may be reproduced in any form or by any means –
graphic, electronic or mechanical, including photocopying, recording, taping
or information storage and retrieval systems – without the written permission
of Bloomsbury Publishing Plc.

This book is produced using paper that is made from wood grown in
managed, sustainable forests. It is natural, renewable and recyclable.
The logging and manufacturing processes conform to the environmental
regulations of the country of origin.

UNIVERSITY OF WINCHESTER

ABOUT THE ROYAL SHAKESPEARE COMPANY

The Royal Shakespeare Company at Stratford-upon-Avon was formed in 1960 and gained its Royal Charter in 1961. This year we celebrate 50 years as a home for Shakespeare's work, the wider classical repertoire and new plays.

The founding Artistic Director, Peter Hall, created an ensemble theatre company of young actors and writers. The Company was led by Hall, Peter Brook and Michel Saint-Denis. The founding principles were threefold: the Company would embrace the freedom and power of Shakespeare's work, train and develop young actors and directors, and crucially, experiment in new ways of making theatre. There was a new spirit amongst this post-war generation and they intended to open up Shakespeare's plays as never before.

The impact of Peter Hall's vision cannot be underplayed. In 1955 he had premiered Samuel Beckett's *Waiting for Godot* in London, and the result was like opening a window during a storm. The tumult of new ideas emerging across Europe in art, theatre and literature came flooding into British theatre. Hall channelled this new excitement into the setting up of the Company in Stratford. Exciting breakthroughs took place in the rehearsal room and the studio day after day. The RSC became known for exhilarating performances of Shakespeare alongside new masterpieces such as *The Homecoming* and *Old Times* by Harold Pinter. It was a combination that thrilled audiences.

Peter Hall's rigour on classical text became legendary, but what is little known is that he applied everything he learned working on Beckett, and later on Harold Pinter, to his work on Shakespeare, and likewise he applied everything he learned from Shakespeare onto modern texts. This close and exacting relationship between writers from different eras became the fuel which powered the creativity of the RSC.

The search for new forms of writing and directing was led by Peter Brook. He pushed writers to experiment. "Just as Picasso set out to capture a larger slice of the truth by painting a face with several eyes and noses, Shakespeare, knowing that man is living his everyday life and at the same time is living intensely in the invisible world of his thoughts and feelings, developed a method through which we can see at one and the same time the look on a man's face and the vibrations of his brain."

A rich and varied range of writers flowed into the company and continue to do so. These include: Edward Albee, Howard Barker, Edward Bond, Howard Brenton, Marina Carr, Caryl Churchill, Martin Crimp, David Edgar, Peter Flannery, David Greig, Tony Harrison, Dennis Kelly, Martin McDonagh, Rona Munro, Anthony Neilson, Harold Pinter, Stephen Poliakoff, Adriano Shaplin, Wole Soyinka, Tom Stoppard, debbie tucker green, Timberlake Wertenbaker and Roy Williams.

The Company today is led by Michael Boyd, who is taking its founding ideals forward. His belief in ensemble theatre-making, internationalism, new work and active approaches to Shakespeare in the classroom has inspired the Company to landmark projects such as *The Complete Works Festival*, *Stand up for Shakespeare* and *The Histories Cycle*. He has overseen the four year transformation of our theatres, he has restored the full range of repertoire and in this birthday year we are proud to invite the world's theatre artists onto our brand new stages.

The RSC New Work season at Hampstead Theatre is generously supported by THE BLAVATNIK FAMILY FOUNDATION

The RSC Literary Department is generously supported by THE DRUE HEINZ TRUST

The RSC Ensemble is generously supported by THE GATSBY CHARITABLE FOUNDATION and THE KOVNER FOUNDATION

The RSC is grateful for the significant support of its principal funder, Arts Council England, without which our work would not be possible. Around 50 per cent of the RSC's income is self-generated from Box Office sales, sponsorship, donations, enterprise and partnerships with other organisations.

Supported by
ARTS COUNCIL ENGLAND

NEW WORK AT THE RSC

We have between thirty and forty writers working on new plays for us at any one time and have recently re-launched the RSC Studio to provide the resources for writers, directors and actors to explore and develop new ideas for our stages. We also explore the canon for classics to revive and lost classics to re-discover.

We invite writers to spend time with us in our rehearsal rooms, with our actors and practitioners. Alongside developing their own plays, we invite them to contribute dramaturgically to both our main stage Shakespeare productions and our Young People's Shakespeare.

We believe that our writers help to establish a creative culture within the Company which both inspires new work and creates an ever more urgent sense of enquiry into the classics. The benefits work both ways. With our writers, our actors naturally learn the language of dramaturgical intervention and sharpen their interpretation of roles. Our writers benefit from re-discovering the stagecraft and theatre skills that have been lost over time. They regain the knack of writing roles for leading actors. They become hungry to use classical structures to power up their plays.

Our current International Writer-in-Residence, Tarell Alvin McCraney, has been embedded with the company for two years. His post was funded by the CAPITAL Centre at the University of Warwick where he taught as part of his residency.

We have a long history of working with experimental theatremakers and our writers are free to choose how they develop their work. They regularly work collaboratively with actors, makers, composers and designers in the rehearsal room to create new work, often with fresh and startling results.

FILTER

Since 2003 Filter has been bringing together actors, musicians, directors, designers, writers and technicians to create innovative, exciting theatre. Filter's unique collaborative language explores the interaction between sound and music, text and movement, in a desire to make stories that truly awaken the imaginative senses of an audience. Working out of a real sense of trust, and retaining a robust emotional honesty and playfulness, Filter tackles new works of original theatre, as well as dynamic incarnations of existing texts.

Filter's first show *Faster*, inspired by James Gleick's book about the acceleration of everyday life in the modern world, was developed and first performed at the Battersea Arts Centre in April 2003, where it was a runaway hit with audiences. *Faster* also played the Soho Theatre, the Lyric Hammersmith, toured the UK and visited Germany and New York.

Examples of Filter's dynamic and innovative interpretations of classic texts are Brecht's *Caucasian Chalk Circle* for the National Theatre; Shakespeare's *Twelfth Night* for the RSC and the Tricycle Theatre; and Chekhov's *Three Sisters* for the Lyric Hammersmith. Each project aspired to pin-point the very heart of the plays by uncovering the light and darkness of the language and the lyricism of the text. With *Caucasian Chalk Circle* Filter's approach was to create a modern and playful production out of Brecht's didacticism, true to the playwright's vision. Filter's production of *Three Sisters* featured a stripped-away design and robust ensemble acting that highlighted the timelessness of the writing; and Filter's radical and riotous interpretation of Shakespeare's *Twelfth Night* reflected the anarchic energy running throughout the play.

Water, directed by David Farr for the Lyric, became one of the most talked about productions of 2007 and was revived at the Tricycle in 2011. *Water* is an intimate, multi-sensory and highly charged piece of theatrical story-telling, exploring deeply personal narratives on two very different issues – the bonds and ties of fathers and sons, and the legacy of global warming.

To find out more about Filter visit **www.filtertheatre.com**

Artistic Directors	**Oliver Dimsdale, Tim Phillips, Ferdy Roberts**
Producer	**Simon Reade**
Financial Manager	**Daniel Morgenstern**
Associate Artists	**Tom Haines, Gemma Saunders**

This production of *Silence* was first performed by the
Royal Shakespeare Company at Hampstead Theatre, London,
on 12th May 2011. The cast was as follows:

MICHAEL	**Oliver Dimsdale**
NATASHA	**Christine Entwisle**
MARY/IRINA	**Mariah Gale**
IVAN	**Paul Hamilton**
NIKOLAS	**Richard Katz**
PETER	**Jonjo O'Neill**
ALEXEI	**Ferdy Roberts**
KENNETH/JOSEF	**Patrick Romer**
KATE	**Katy Stephens**

All other parts played by members of the Company.

Directed by	**David Farr**
Designed by	**Jon Bausor**
Lighting Designed by	**Jon Clark**
Music and Sound by	**Tim Phillips**
Video Designed by	**Douglas O'Connell**
Dialect Coach	**Charmian Hoare**
Assistant Director	**Justin Audibert**
Casting by	**Hannah Miller** cᴅɢ
Production Manager	**Rebecca Watts**
Costume Supervisor	**Laura Hunt**
Company Manager	**Michael Dembowicz**
Stage Manager	**Pip Horobin**
Deputy Stage Manager	**Juliette Taylor**
Assistant Stage Manager	**Joanna Vimpany**

This text may differ slightly from the play as performed.

Production Acknowledgments

The co-creators of *Silence* would like to thank Susan Richards for her inspirational book *Lost and Found in Russia*, published by I.B. Tauris & Co. Ltd.

Set and scenic art by Capital Scenery, London. Props and settings by RSC workshops, Stratford-upon-Avon. Dances choreographed by Ann Yee. With thanks to Mark Franchetti, Gail Gallie, Olly Lambert, Owen Matthews, Joshua Neale, Carey Scott, Vassily Skorik, Masha Slomon, Alice Terekhova. Production photographer Simon Kane. Audio description by Carolyn Smith and Ridanne Sheridan. Captioned by Janet Jackson.

THE COMPANY

Justin Audibert

ASSISTANT DIRECTOR

RSC: *Twelfth Night, Future Regrets* (Live Theatre, Newcastle).

Ensemble productions: *Morte d'Arthur, Julius Caesar, Silence.*

trained: Arts Council MFA in Theatre Directing at Birkbeck.

theatre includes: As assistant director: *And the Horse You Rode in On* (Told By An Idiot); *Peter Pan, Fast Labour, The Grouch, Runaway Diamonds, Beauty and the Beast* (West Yorkshire Playhouse). Other work includes: *Casanova* (Told by an Idiot/UK tour/Lyric Hammersmith); *Where's Vietnam* (40th anniversary production. Red Ladder); *A Month in the Country, Nana* (ArtsEd, London). Directing includes: *Measure for Measure, Twelfth Night, Kings Cross Voices* (ArtsEd, London); *Company Along the Mile* (West Yorkshire Playhouse/Arcola/The Lowry); *Armley: the Musical* (Interplay/I Love West Leeds Festival); *Born Abroad* (West Yorkshire Playhouse); *Trinity's Saint, Ready Mades* (West Yorkshire Playhouse/Leeds Light Night 2007). Justin is a selector for the National Student Drama Festival (NSDF) and a residency director on Told by an Idiot's Taught by an Idiot Programme.

Jon Bausor

DESIGNER

RSC: *Julius Caesar* (as actor).

Ensemble productions: *The Winter's Tale, King Lear, Silence.*

trained: Motley Theatre design course and Oxford University.

theatre includes: *Sanctuary, The Tempest* (National Theatre); *Baghdad Wedding* (Soho); *The Birthday Party* (Lyric Hammersmith); *Water* (Filter/Lyric Hammersmith); *Romeo and Juliet, Terminus, Big Love* (Abbey, Dublin); *Macbeth, Cymbeline* (Regent's Park Open Air Theatre); *In the Bag, Night Time* (Traverse); *The Soldier's Tale* (Old Vic); *James and the Giant Peach* (Bolton Octagon); *Scenes from the Back of Beyond* (Royal Court); *Direct Action season, The Soul of Chien-nu* (Young Vic); *The Taming of the Shrew* (Thelma Holt/Theatre Royal, Plymouth).

opera includes: *The Knot Garden* (Klangbogen, Vienna); *Queen of Spades* (Edinburgh Festival Theatre); *The Lighthouse* (Theatro Poliziano, Montepulciano).

dance includes: *The Thief of Baghdad, Ghosts, Before the Tempest* (Royal Opera House); *A Tale of Two Cities* (Northern Ballet); *Scribblings* (Rambert); *Firebird* (Stradttheater, Bern); *Snow White in Black* (Phoenix Dance); *Non Exeunt* (Ballet Boyz/George Piper Dances); *Mixtures* (ENB).

Jon Clark

LIGHTING DESIGNER

RSC: *The Merchant of Venice.*

Ensemble productions: *The Winter's Tale, King Lear, Silence.*

trained: Bretton Hall, University of Leeds.

theatre includes: *Hamlet, Greenland, Beauty and the Beast, The Cat in the Hat, Pains of Youth, Our Class, Moonlight, Polar Bears* (Donmar); *Red Bud, Aunt Dan and Lemon, The Pride, Gone Too Far!* (Royal Court); *Into the Woods* (Open Air, Regent's Park); *Been So Long, The Jewish Wife, How Much is Your Iron?* (Young Vic); *Salome* (Headlong); *The Little Dog Laughed* (Garrick); *Three Days of Rain* (Apollo. Knight of Illumination Award for Best Lighting Design and Olivier nomination for Best Lighting Design); *The Lover and The Collection, Dickens Unplugged* (Comedy); *The Birthday Party, Spyski!, Water* (Lyric Hammersmith); *Eric's* (Liverpool Everyman); *On the Rocks* (Hampstead); *Ghosts* (ATC/Arcola).

opera includes: *The Return of Ulysses (ENO); Clemency (ROH2); The Lion's Face, Into the Little Hill, Recital, Down by the Greenwood Side, Street Scene* (The Opera Group); *The Love for Three Oranges* (Scottish Opera/RSAMD); *I Capuleti e I Montecchi, L'Elisir d'Amore, The Barber of Seville, Così Fan Tutte* (Grange Park Opera).

dance includes: *Will Tuckett's Pleasure's Progress* (ROH2/DanceEast); *Cathy Marston's Clara, Libera Me, Karole Armitage's Between the Clock & The Bed, Andrea Miller's Howl* (Bern Ballett); *Lay Me Down Safe, Tenderhook, Sorry for the Missiles* (Scottish Dance Theatre); *Anton & Erin - Cheek to Cheek* (London Coliseum).

Oliver Dimsdale

MICHAEL

RSC: *Twelfth Night* (Filter/RSC), *The Tempest* (UK/world tour).
this season: Michael in *Silence*.
Oliver is a co-founder and co-Artistic Director of Filter Theatre.
theatre includes: *Water* (Filter/Lyric Hammersmith/Tricycle); *Pravda* (Birmingham Rep/Chichester Festival); *Caucasian Chalk Circle* (Filter/National Theatre); *The Creeper* (West End/tour); *The Comedy of Errors* (Sheffield Crucible); *The Dead Wait* (MEN Award Best Fringe Performer), *Great Expectations* (Manchester Royal Exchange); *Faster* (BAC/Lyric/New York); *Workers Writes* (Royal Court); *A Midsummer Night's Dream* (Wild Thyme); *Beautiful*

Thing, The Changeling, Five Finger Exercise (Salisbury Playhouse).
television includes: *Law and Order UK, Breaking the Mould, Harley Street, Larkrise to Candleford, Fallen Angel, He Knew He was Right, Byron, Dalziel and Pascoe, Inspector Lynley Mysteries, Casualty, Doctors.*
film includes: *What You Will, First Night, Rocknrolla, Nostradamus, Pest, Soho Story.*
radio includes: *Sharp Focus, In the Company of Men.*

Christine Entwisle

NATASHA

Ensemble productions: Phoebe in *As You Like It*, Adriana in *The Comedy of Errors*, Mayor's Aide in *The Drunks*, Lady Capulet in *Romeo and Juliet*, Margawse in *Morte d'Arthur*, Natasha in *Silence*.
theatre includes: *Six Characters in Search of an Author* (Gielgud/Headlong/Chichester); *Half Life* (National Theatre of Scotland); *The Wonderful World of Dissocia* (Royal Court/National Theatre of Scotland); *Duckie, C'est Vauxhall* (Barbican); *Vassa* (Almeida/Albery); *A Family Affair* (Theatr Clwyd); *Wonderhorse* (Edinburgh

Festival/ICA/BAC); *Edward Gant* (Theatre Royal, Plymouth); *I Am Dandy* (Purcell Rooms/BAC); *Ubu Kunst, Missing Jesus, Fine* (Young Vic); *People Shows 100-103* (International tour); *The Wedding, Paper Walls* (Scarlet Theatre).
television and film includes: *Attachments, Holby City, Mothers and Daughters, At Dawning, A&E, Where the Heart Is, Dalziel and Pascoe, Storm Damages, Deeper Still.*
radio: *Heredity.*
writing/directing includes: Film: *Our Ordered Lives, Death of a Double Act, Bat Boy, Relate* (North West Vision and Media, UK Film Council). Theatre: *Missing Jesus, Fine, Perilous Stuff* (Young Vic); *Genetics for Blondes* (Soho). Cabaret: *Lady Witherslack, Clare Voyant, Wonderhorse.*

David Farr

DIRECTOR

RSC: Associate Director. *Coriolanus, Julius Caesar, Night of the Soul.*
Ensemble productions: *King Lear, The Winter's Tale, Silence.*
From 2005 to 2008 David was the Artistic Director of the Lyric Theatre, Hammersmith. He was joint Artistic Director of Bristol Old Vic from 2002 to 2005 and Artistic Director of the Gate Theatre, London, from 1995 to 1998. He has also directed at The National Theatre, The Young Vic and the National Theatre of Czech Republic.

theatre includes: *The Odyssey, Metamorphosis, Water* (with Filter Theatre); *The Resistible Rise of Arturo Ui, The Birthday Party* (Lyric Hammersmith); *Tamburlaine* (Barbican); *The UN Inspector* (National Theatre); *Paradise Lost, Twelfth Night, A Midsummer Night's Dream* (TMA Best Director Award. Bristol Old Vic). Playwriting includes: *The Nativity* (Young Vic); *The Danny Crowe Show* (Bush); *Elton John's Glasses* (Watford Palace/West End); *Crime and Punishment in Dalston* (Arcola); *Night of the Soul, The Queen Must Die, Ruckus in the Garden* (National Theatre Connections).

television: David writes regularly for the television series *Spooks*.

film writing includes: *Hanna* directed by Joe Wright (2011).

Mariah Gale

RSC: *A Midsummer Night's Dream, Hamlet* (special commendation, Ian Charleson Award 2008), *Love's Labour's Lost, Antony and Cleopatra, Julius Caesar, The Tempest.*

Ensemble productions:
Celia in *As You Like It* (special commendation, Ian Charleson Award 2009), Courtesan in *The Comedy of Errors*, Masha in *The Grain Store*, Juliet in *Romeo and Juliet,* Lady Ettard/Elaine in *Morte d'Arthur,* Mary/Irina in *Silence*.

trained: Guildhall School of Music and Drama.

theatre includes: *The Sea* (Theatre Royal Haymarket); *Vernon God Little* (Young Vic); *'Tis Pity She's a Whore* (Critics' Circle Award for Most Promising Newcomer 2005. Time Out Live award for Best Newcomer 2005. First prize Ian Charleson Award 2005. Southwark Playhouse); *Cymbeline, Twelfth Night* (Regent's Park); *Professor Bernhardi, Musik* (Arcola); *Much Ado About Nothing* (Shakespeare's Globe); *The Lost Child* (Chichester); *Stealing Sweets and Punching People* (Latchmere).

television includes: *The Diary of Anne Frank, Oliver Twist, Skins*.

film: *Abraham's Point, Hamlet*.

radio includes: *Parthenogenesis, Regime Change, Brian Gulliver's Travels*.

Paul Hamilton

RSC: *The Histories Cycle, Troilus and Cressida, The Mysteries, Everyman.*

Ensemble productions:
Servant in *The Winter's Tale*, Caius Ligarius/Messala in *Julius Caesar*, 3rd Passenger/2nd Barfly in *The Drunks*, Knight/Cornwall's Man in *King Lear*, Diomedes in *Antony and Cleopatra*, Ivan in *Silence.*

theatre includes: *Elizabeth* (Kabosh Theatre); *Peri Banez* (Young Vic); *The Story of Yours* (New End); *Of Mice and Men, A View from the Bridge* (Harrogate); *A Streetcar Named Desire* (Royal Lyceum); *The Crucible, Mensch Meier, Blood Wedding, Under Milk Wood* (Haymarket, Leicester); *The Southwark Mysteries* (Shakespeare's Globe); *Three Lives of Lucie Cabrol* (Complicite); *Out of a House Walked a Man* (Complicite/National Theatre); *The Tale of Yvaine* (Royal Festival Hall); *Gormenghast* (David Glass Ensemble); *Crimes of Passion* (Nottingham Playhouse); *Northern Trawl* (Hull Truck).

television includes: *55 Degrees North, Heartbeat, The Long Firm, Emmerdale, Badger, Henry IV Parts 1 and 2, Pie in the Sky, Never the Sinner*.

film includes: *The Gathering, Bridget Jones' Diary, A Dinner of Herbs*.

Richard Katz

NIKOLAS

RSC: *The Winter's Tale, Pericles*.

Ensemble productions: Touchstone in *As You Like It*, Antipholus of Syracuse in *The Comedy of Errors*, Sergey in *The Drunks*, Capulet in *Romeo and Juliet*, King Pellinor/ Cardinal Bishop of Rochester/ Baudwin of Britayne in *Morte d'Arthur*, Nikolas in *Silence*.

theatre includes: *Spyski!* (Lyric Hammersmith/ Peepolykus); *How to Tell the Monsters from the Misfits* (Birmingham Rep); *Señora Carrar's Rifles, Arabian Nights* (Young Vic); *Way to Heaven* (Royal Court); *Faustus* (Northampton); *Measure for Measure* (National Theatre/Complicite); *Life Game* (National Theatre/ Improbable); *Strange Poetry, The Noise of Time, Mnemonic* (Complicite); *The Hanging Man, Angela Carter's*

Cinderella (Improbable/ Lyric Hammersmith); *The Golden Ass, A Midsummer Night's Dream* (Shakespeare's Globe); *Genoa 01* (Royal Court/Complicite).

television includes: *Review of the Year 2009, Thank God You're Here, MI High, The Site, The Passion, Hogfather, The Omid Djalili Show, Green Wing, Hyperdrive, Hustle, Absolute Power, Rome, Nicholas Nickleby*.

film includes: *Measure for Measure, Sixty Six, Start, Enigma, The Last Sin*.

radio includes: *Marley Was Dead, Apes and Angels, The Archers, The Grand Babylon Hotel, Beat the Dog in His Own Kennel*.

writing for radio: *Marley Was Dead, The Newbury Arms*.

Douglas O'Connell

VIDEO DESIGNER

RSC DEBUT SEASON: *Silence*.

Currently Douglas is MA Course Director for Visual Language of Performance at The University Arts London, Wimbledon and lectures in digital performance at the Central School of Speech and Drama.

theatre includes: *Frankenstein, Frankie and Johnny* (Steppenwolf Theatre, Chicago); *Invertigo* (Lewisham); *Here's What I did with my Body One Day* (national tour); *Saturday Night, Sunday Morning* (Harrogate); *Sarajevo Story, Fight Face*

(Lyric Hammersmith); *Back at You* (BAC); *This Isn't Romance* (Soho); *Monsters* (Arcola); *Behud* (Belgrade, Coventry); *Ballet Shoes* (Children's Ballet, London), Bluemouth Inc's, *Dance Marathon* (Vancouver Olympics/ international tour).

other: Douglas has developed numerous online research performance projects to support his ongoing research in online digital performance, in which he received a fellowship for Promising New Research from the AHRC. His multi-media work has featured at the Visions Festival in Brighton, The National Theatre's Festival of Lights, The Greenwich Council, The National Youth Theatre Conference, as well as the [re]actor Conference on Digital Live Art. He has led site-specific projects with Birmingham Royal Ballet, Emergency Exit Arts, and the Greenwich/Dockland Festival.

Jonjo O'Neill

PETER

RSC: *Head/Case, Believe What You Will, A New Way to Please You, Sejanus: His Fall, Speaking Like Magpies*.

Ensemble productions: Orlando in *As You Like It*,

Dromio of Syracuse in *The Comedy of Errors*, Ilya in *The Drunks*, Mercutio in *Romeo and Juliet*, Launcelot in *Morte d'Arthur*, Peter in *Silence*.
theatre includes: *King Lear* (Liverpool Everyman/Young Vic); *Someone Else's Shoes* (Soho); *Faustus* (Hampstead); *Paradise Lost* (Northampton Theatre Royal); *A View from the Bridge, The David Hare Trilogy* (Birmingham Rep); *Observe the Sons of Ulster* (Pleasance); *Dolly West's Kitchen* (Haymarket, Leicester); *Half a Sixpence* (West Yorkshire Playhouse); *Translations* (Watford Palace/tour); *Dick Whittington* (Sadler's Wells); *Of Thee I Sing* (Bridewell Theatre); *The Frogs* (Nottingham Playhouse/tour); *Refuge* (Royal Court).
television includes: *The History of Mr Polly, I Do, The Year London Blew Up, I Fought the Law, Bay College, Murphy's Law: Manic Monday, A Touch of Frost, Charlie's Angel, Band of Brothers, Holby City, Thin Ice, Extremely Dangerous, Sunburn, Risk.*
film includes: *Defiance, Fakers.*

Tim Phillips

MUSIC AND SOUND
RSC DEBUT SEASON:
Silence.
Tim is a composer, songwriter, and producer with studios in New York and London.
theatre includes: Tim is co-founder and co-Artistic

Director of Filter. In addition to Filter shows, Tim has written scores for many plays, most recently for *A Doll's House* at the Donmar Warehouse and *Juliet and her Romeo* at Bristol Old Vic (with Marc Teitler). He is also currently developing a musical, *Burn Me Dead*, as well as several upcoming Filter shows.
television includes: Tim has written music for many screen productions including HBO's *Entourage*, Company Pictures' *Talk to Me*, and Tightrope Pictures' RTS award-winning *Instinct*. He has also scored the last 6 series of C4's smash hit *Shameless*. He is currently working on *Satisfaction*, a television series he created with the writer John-Henry Butterworth under their joint venture Eat Me Productions.
other: His new album of songs, *The Armstrong Tapes*, will be released in 2011.

Ferdy Roberts

ALEXEI
RSC: *Twelfth Night* (RSC/Filter).
this season: Alexei in *Silence.*
Ferdy is a co-founder and co-Artistic Director of Filter Theatre and an

Associate Artist at the Lyric, Hammersmith.
theatre includes: For Filter: *Three Sisters* (Lyric Hammersmith/tour); *Twelfth Night* (Tricycle Theatre/tour); *Water* (Lyric Hammersmith/tour); *The Caucasian Chalk Circle* (National Theatre/tour); *Faster* (London/New York). Other theatre: *Wallenstein* (Chichester Festival); *On Religion* (Theatre Poche, Brussels); *The Birthday Party, The Dumb Waiter*, Aladdin (Bristol Old Vic); *Frankenstein* (Derby Playhouse); *Another Country* (West End); *Rise And Fall Of Little Voice, The Changeling, Beautiful Thing* (Salisbury Playhouse).
television includes: *Mi High, Whistleblower, The Bill, Goldplated, Your Mother Should Know, Holby City.*
film includes: *What You Will, Mr Nice, Sex, Drugs and Rock & Roll, Honest.*

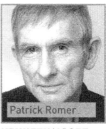
Patrick Romer

KENNETH/JOSEF
RSC: *Much Ado about Nothing, Romeo and Juliet, Julius Caesar, The Two Gentlemen of Verona, The Merry Wives of Windsor, Coriolanus.*
Ensemble productions: Time/Mariner/Gaoler/Servant

in *The Winter's Tale*, Murullus/
Publius/Cinna, the Poet/Clitus
in *Julius Caesar*, Artiukh the
Burier/Old Woman Dancing
in *The Grain Store*, Ghost/A
Player/Gravedigger/Pirate
in *Hamlet*, Cousin Capulet/
Apothecary/Constable in
Romeo and Juliet, Archbishop
of Canterbury/Nacien the
Hermit in *Morte d'Arthur*,
Kenneth/Josef in *Silence*.
trained: Rose Bruford.
theatre includes: *The
Masque of the Red Death*
(Punchdrunk); *Bulletproof
Soul* (Birmingham Rep); *The
Comedy of Errors* (Bristol Old
Vic); *Mirita* (Finborough); *La
Cava* (Piccadilly); *An Enemy
of the People, Peter Pan*
(National Theatre); *The Tailor-
Made Man* (Cockpit); *Of Mice
and Men* (Coventry Belgrade);
The Cid, Twelfth Night (Cheek
by Jowl/tour). Patrick has
also been involved in over 60
productions for the Northcott
Theatre, Exeter and over 12
productions for the Lyceum
Theatre, Crewe.
television includes:
*Primeval, Robinson Crusoe,
The Four Seasons, Casualty,
The Bill, The Project, DDU*.
film: *The World is Not
Enough*.
radio includes: *All Passion
Spent*, regular reader on
Poetry Please, reader for
RNIB's talking books.

Katy Stephens

KATE

RSC: *The Histories Cycle*.
Ensemble productions:
Rosalind in *As You Like It*,
Samoilenka in *The Grain
Store*, Regan in *King Lear*,
Cleopatra in *Antony and
Cleopatra*, Kate in *Silence*.
trained: National Youth
Theatre, Welsh College of
Music and Drama.
theatre includes:
Tamburlaine (Bristol Old Vic/
Barbican); *The Seagull, Ion,
Macbeth, The White Devil,
Oh! What a Lovely War, The
Three Sisters, The Europeans,
Caucasian Chalk Circle, Blood
Wedding, The Recruiting
Officer* (Mercury, Colchester);
*Twelfth Night, Sleeping Beauty,
Our Day Out, Silas Marner*
(Belgrade, Coventry); *David
Copperfield, I Don't Want
to Set the World on Fire*
(New Victoria, Newcastle); *A
Midsummer Night's Dream*
(Orchard Theatre Co.).
television includes: *The Bill,
London's Burning, Ellington,
Fun Song Factory, Wow*.
film: *Relative Values*.

FOR THE RSC AT HAMPSTEAD

Jennifer Binns
Wardrobe Mistress

Katie Brooks
Props Supervisor

Lydia Cassidy
London Marketing Consultant

Réjane Collard
Literary Assistant

David Collins
Head of Marketing

Kevin Fitzmaurice
Season Producer

Craig Garratt
Senior Sound Technician

Robin Griggs
Lighting Technician

Philippa Harland
Head of Press

Chris Hill
Director of Sales and Marketing

Pippa Hill
Literary Manager

Mig Kimpton
London Manager

Katie Marsh
*London Press and
Marketing Assistant*

Fiona Matthews
Wigs & Make-up Mistress

Hannah Miller
Head of Casting

Miwa Mitsuhashi
Wardrobe Assistant

Helena Palmer
Casting Director

Keshini Ranasinghe
Dresser

Lauren Rubery
*London Facilities and
Operations Administrator*

Janine Snape
Assistant Casting Director

Kate Stokes
Senior Stage Technician

Robert Weatherhead
Senior Props Technician

Richard Williamson
Senior Lighting Technician

Marketing, Sales and Advertising
AKA Marketing (020 7836 4747)

JOIN US

Join us from £18 a year.

Join today and make a difference
The Royal Shakespeare Company is an ensemble. We perform all year round in our Stratford-upon-Avon home, as well as having regular seasons in London, and touring extensively within the UK and overseas for international residencies.

With a range of options from £18 to £10,000 per year, there are many ways to engage with the RSC.

Choose a level that suits you and enjoy a closer connection with us whilst also supporting our work on stage.

Find us online
Sign up for regular email updates at **www.rsc.org.uk/signup**

Join today
Annual RSC Full Membership costs just £40 (or £18 for Associate Membership) and provides you with regular updates on RSC news, advance information and priority booking.

Support us
A charitable donation from £100 a year can offer you the benefits of membership, whilst also allowing you the opportunity to deepen your relationship with the Company through special events, backstage tours and exclusive ticket booking services.

The options include Shakespeare's Circle (from £100), Patrons' Circle (Silver: £1,000, Gold: £5,000) and Artists' Circle (£10,000).

For more information visit **www.rsc.org.uk/joinus** or call the RSC Membership Office on 01789 403 440.

THE ROYAL SHAKESPEARE COMPANY

Patron
Her Majesty the Queen

President
His Royal Highness The Prince of Wales

Deputy President
Sir Geoffrey Cass

Artistic Director
Michael Boyd

Executive Director
Vikki Heywood

Board
Sir Christopher Bland (*Chairman*)
Professor Jonathan Bate CBE FBA FRSL
Michael Boyd (*Artistic Director*)
Damon Buffini
David Burbidge OBE
Jane Drabble OBE
Noma Dumezweni
Mark Foster
Gilla Harris
Vikki Heywood (*Executive Director*)
John Hornby
Baroness McIntosh of Hudnall
Paul Morrell OBE
Tim Pigott-Smith
Neil Rami
Lady Sainsbury of Turville (*Deputy Chairman*)

The RSC was established in 1961. It is incorporated under Royal Charter and is a registered charity, number 212481.

Hampstead Theatre is one of the UK's leading new writing companies – a company that has just celebrated its fiftieth year of operation.

Throughout its long history the theatre has existed to support a thriving local, national and international playwriting culture. We commission plays in order to enrich and enliven this culture. We support, develop and produce the work of new writers, emerging writers, established writers, mid-career writers and senior writers and have a proud tradition for creating the conditions for their plays and careers to develop.

The list of playwrights who had their early work produced at Hampstead Theatre and who are now filling theatres all over the country and beyond include Mike Leigh, Michael Frayn, Brian Friel, Terry Johnson, Hanif Kureishi, Simon Block, Abi Morgan, Rona Munro, Tamsin Oglesby, Harold Pinter, Shelagh Stephenson, debbie tucker green, Crispin Whittell, Roy Williams and Dennis Kelly.

The Creative Learning programme is also an integral part of Hampstead Theatre's work. We aim to celebrate all aspects of the creative process in ways which support learning and widen access to the theatre's programme. Inspiring creativity and developing emerging talent, at its best our work has the power to change lives.

In January 2010, Edward Hall was appointed Artistic Director of Hampstead Theatre. Hall's inaugural season was a box office   culminating in a West End transfer of Mike Leigh's revival of *Ecstasy*. Hampstead Theatre looks forward to welcoming the RSC and Hall's own company, the internationally acclaimed Propeller, over the forthcoming months.

Hampstead Downstairs was opened in November 2010. It seats 98 and stages raw, edgy and experimental work. The audience decide for themselves what they think of the work, with their decisions not being predetermined by media reviews. Previous productions include *small hours* directed by Katie Mitchell and *.45* written by Gary Lennon.

Hall's second season, autumn 2011, will continue to delight, inspire and engage with such directors as Katie Mitchell, Richard Eyre and Roger Michell taking to the stage.

Hampstead Theatre, Eton Avenue, Swiss Cottage, London NW3 3EU

www.hampsteadtheatre.com

Supported by
**ARTS COUNCIL
ENGLAND**

Registered charity number: 218506

Silence

UNIVERSITY OF WINCHESTER
LIBRARY

Characters

Kate
Nikolas
Alexei
Michael
Peter
Mary
Kenneth
BBC Producer
Sophie
Natasha
Ivan
Josef
Irina
BBC Sound Guy

Prologue

Irina, *a Russian woman, thirty-one years old, posts an envelope in a small town in Russia, in 2010.*

In London, **Kate** *receives the same envelope in the post. Alone on stage, she turns to talk to us.*

Kate   I have a ringing in my ears. I've had it since I was a child. It's a high-pitched whine, comes and goes, sometimes it makes me dizzy, sometimes it makes me sick. My brain imagines sound where there isn't any. So quiet doesn't help. Instead I have filled my life with more noise to get rid of it. Music, clubs, television, the chatter of people –

Enter **Michael**.

Michael   Hey!

Kate   – my husband's voice. It's ringing as I speak to you now. It was ringing when I made love to my husband Michael in our Battersea apartment this morning. It was ringing when the post arrived. It was ringing when I found this letter amongst the bills and bank statements. I recognised the writing on the envelope.

Out of the envelope she takes a tape.

Scene One

BATTERSEA INTO BERLIN

Kate *and* **Michael** *in Battersea, London, 2010,* **Kate** *holding the tape which she has just received in the post.*

Now, a memory: **Kate**, *twenty-three years old, meets* **Nikolas**, *also early twenties, in a club in Berlin in 1991. They struggle to hear each other.*

Nikolas   *Wo ist ihr name?*

Kate   What?

Nikolas   *Wo ist ihr name?*

Kate   I don't speak German.

Nikolas (*Russian accent*)   What do you speak?

Kate   Are you Russian?

Nikolas (*Russian accent*)   Yes!

Kate   I can speak Russian!

Nikolas   You speak Russian!

Kate   Yes! My grandmother is from Russia. Why do you smell of fish?

Nikolas   My friend and I drove twenty-seven hours in a car full of sturgeon to get here.

Kate   What?

Nikolas   Sturgeon. The only currency of choice between here and Moscow!

Kate   Why are you in Berlin?

Nikolas   Research trip! We have a club in Moscow. The Travel Bureau.

Kate   The what?

Nikolas   The Travel Bureau! We come here, we buy music, be part of the scene!

Kate   'We'?

Nikolas   Me and my friend. Alexei. He has to go to army in two weeks!

Kate   To what?

Nikolas   To army. National service! So this is his last party!

Kate   We say in England 'Last Supper'!

Nikolas   'Last Supper'! I like it!

Kate   Where is he?

Nikolas   You'll know him when you see him. He's the only one here with a beard! The last beard in Russia!

He takes out a pill.

Nikolas   You want one?

He holds out a pill. **Kate** *has tinnitus moment.*

Kate   What?

Nikolas (*offering her pill*)   Do you want one?

Kate   How do I know you're not the Stazi?!

Nikolas   This is 1991! There haven't been any Stazi in Berlin since the Wall came down.

Kate   What? Speak up!

Nikolas   No Stazi!

Kate *takes the pill.*

And the music fades up.

She gets an attack of the tinnitus.

In the chaos **Kate** *sees* **Alexei** *on the dance floor, staring at her.*

Her tinnitus disappears.

She stands there looking at him. They hear each other's thoughts.

Alexei   You OK?

Kate   Yeah.

Alexei   You want to get out of here?

Kate   Yeah.

Alexei *is holding out two Sony Walkmans.* **Kate** *puts the tape in the Walkman. He puts his tape in his Walkman.*

And we are in a sleepy early-morning Berlin U-Bahn carriage in 1991.

Alexei   Ready?

Kate (*excitedly, a whisper*)   No!

Alexei   One. Two.

Kate *kisses him.*

Alexei   Three!

And they both press 'play'. Silence for a second and then the screech of Little Richard's 'Rip It Up' roars into life.

And **Kate** *and* **Alexei** *dance like mad people in the U-Bahn, surprising and pleasing the fellow travellers. Until, on the U-Bahn's Tannoy:*

Tannoy   Alexanderplatz, Alexanderplatz . . .

Kate *looks at her watch.*

Kate   Oh no. Oh God, I've got to get off!

Alexei   Why?

Kate   My flight's from Tegel in an hour. I have to go.

The U-Bahn is stopping at the station. **Kate** *gets out on to the platform.*

Alexei   Come to Moscow.

Pause.

Come to Moscow.

Kate   I can't.

Alexei   Nikolas and I are driving back this afternoon. Berlin, Cracow, Lodz, Moscow.

Kate *looks at him. The doors are about to close.*

She leaps back on to the U-Bahn train. Kisses him.

Alexei *disappears as she kisses him and* **Kate** *is left back in her kitchen in Battersea in 2010 with the tape in her hand. She puts the tape back in the envelope.*

Michael *is in the kitchen.*

Michael   What was that?

Kate   Nothing.

Michael   Come back to bed.

Kate   . . .

Michael   You can be an hour late.

Kate   Says you, the workaholic.

Michael   Come on.

They kiss.

Kate   . . .

Michael   What is it?

Kate   I think I may have to go to Moscow.

Michael   Moscow?

Kate   Yeah.

Michael   When

Kate   Today. Now.

Michael   Why?

Pause.

Kate   Nokia.

Michael   Nokia?

Kate   I just got a message on my phone. They're in Moscow anyway for some rebrand, and they've called a crisis meeting. Something about the summer festivals. It's a 400k account.

Michael   Can't someone else go?

Kate   I'd send Tina, but she can't fly.

Michael   Why not?

Kate *mimes pregnancy.*

Michael   Oh yeah.

Kate   It'll only be until Monday.

Michael   Always troubleshooting.

Kate   Yeah.

Michael   Just for a second I thought we were going to have a weekend alone.

Kate   I'm sorry.

Michael   I just thought it was a chance to . . .

Kate   To what?

Michael   To talk. About things.

Kate   What things?

Michael   It's OK.

Kate   No, what things?

Michael   We've been together seven years. We're thirty-eight years old . . .

Kate   You're thirty-eight. I'm still thirty-seven.

Michael   It doesn't matter how old I am.

Pause.

Kate   I thought you didn't want to have this conversation?

Michael   I've changed my mind.

Kate   Look, I need to book my flight. Can we talk about this when I get back?

Michael   Sure.

Kate   I want to. I really want to.

She kisses him passionately, suddenly.

Michael   What was that for?

Kate   So you don't forget me.

Michael   By Monday?

Kate   You're a very popular man.

She kisses him again.

Michael   Monday.

Kate   Monday.

She leaves. **Michael** *sits thinking.* **Peter** *calls.*

Michael   Peter?

Peter   OK, so the Met archive tapes have arrived. Guess how many hours they've sent us?

Michael   Surprise me.

Peter   Six hundred.

Michael   You're joking.

Peter   It's going to take me days, weeks, to get through this . . . I'm going to need some help . . . I know this is your weekend off . . .

Michael   No, actually it's not. Not any more. I'll meet you later at the studio.

He has now got dressed and suddenly turns to us, hanging up the phone.

Scene Two

MICHAEL'S LECTURE

Michael *gives us a brief lecture on the art of documentary to a film school.*

Michael   So how do you become a documentary film-maker? Some people think that anyone can do it. They pick up a camera, the technology's cheap, no real training, they think I want to make a film in X – usually it's a subject in a country where they want to go. Guys always want to go off to conflict zones. I was in Beirut recently and it was just awash with wannabe film-makers, it was hysterical, they were fucking everywhere. They come back to the UK, cut something together, make a trailer, try to interest a broadcaster, fail and nine times out of ten end up on YouTube.

I'm a professional. And the only way to become a professional is to do what you're doing right now. Learn, graft, study, listen to people like me who've already made it. And work.

When I'm talking to film students like you guys, I always say, for the great film, just focus on three things. One – choose the right subject. Make it edgy, dangerous. Ask yourself the question, why now? I'm doing a film at the moment on violence in the London Met under Thatcher's government. Why? Because I can see that all that is coming right back in right now. Riots. Demos. For Poll Tax, read cuts in welfare. For student loans, read student fees. For police violence, read police violence. For Blair Peach read Ian Tomlinson. It's all about what's happening now. Be on the pulse.

Two – when you find someone willing to talk to you, don't charge in. When you call them to meet, suggest a neutral location, somewhere near where they live. Make up a reason you're passing. 'Oh I happen to have an aunt who lives near there. I'm popping round tomorrow to cut her lawn, so I can meet you on the way.' And when you meet, don't scare them. No cameras at first. Just focus on getting into their house, into their life. And then, slowly bring the camera in, bring the microphones. Have a sound guy who's sensitive. No loudmouths, no jokers. My guy, Peter McGuinness, is the best there is.

Three – know when to go for the kill. If the guy is willing to talk, to say something private, secret, personal, then you have a window of twelve hours before he clams up. Do not let that window pass! Push, cajole, lie, anything to keep him talking. Talk for twelve hours if you have to, just to get the six minutes that you need. Those six minutes are your ticket to a prime-time slot on national television.

A very talented editor once told me that to learn how to be a good director, you must learn how to 'Get on a busy commuter train, in the rush hour, with a goat – look everyone in the eye, and not apologise!' I say it differently. When you're making a film, nothing else matters. Life, love, family, forget it. This piece of footage is all that matters.

Pause.

This piece of footage is all that matters.

Scene Three

PETER AND MARY I

Hounslow, 2010. Early morning.

Peter, *the sound recordist, presses 'record'. He takes us on a sound meditation from the most external sounds to the most internal.*

Peter   Peter McGuinness. Friday 11 June 2010.

First planes landing at Heathrow Terminal 2. Lockheed Tristar from Chicago. Boeing 747. New York.

Fire engine leaving Hounslow fire station. Down the A4.

Rush-hour traffic. Dog.

In the house. The radio of the man upstairs.

Elevator in the building – fourteenth floor.

The water in the pipes.

The sound of my breath, the beating of my heart.

He is interrupted by the sounds of the girl next door, waking for her day. Opening the fridge. Listening to the radio. Putting in the toast.

Peter   The girl next door making toast.

Peter *knows exactly how long the toaster lasts before popping. She does the same every day and clearly* **Peter** *has been listening every day.*

The girl leaves her apartment and **Peter** *rushes out also so he can catch the lift with her. He listens to her eating her toast. It's a sound he adores. Then her phone rings.*

Mary   Caroline? . . . Yeah, I'm on first shift, I'll be there at six thirty. Terminal 2, yeah . . . Yeah, I know about that, the guy in Carshalton. Yeah, his suitcase ended up in Nairobi and it's got some fucking kite, for his son's birthday. Yeah, he shouted a lot . . . OK. I'll call him from switchboard . . . No, I'm working tomorrow. And Sunday, yeah . . . Paula's party? . . . Why, are you going? I don't know. I don't think I should . . . Because . . . because . . . We'll see, OK? . . . OK.

They leave the lift and **Peter** *looks up at the flight path. The sound of aeroplanes takes us to . . .*

Scene Four

MOSCOW HOTEL RECEPTION AND ROOM 12

Moscow, 2010. **Kate** *has landed.*

She goes to a hotel that seems to have some significance for her. She is expecting to meet **Alexei**.

Kate   Apologies for my Russian, my name is Kate Rigby, I've just flown in from London . . . I haven't booked a room, I called earlier . . . I'm looking for a man, he's called Alexei Skorik . . . Could you check for me please?

The receptionist types at her keyboard, then shakes her head.

Kate   Are you sure? Definitely? Alexei S-K-O-R-I-K.

No response. **Kate** *turns to exit then turns back.*

Kate   Could you try Room 12? Is there someone in Room 12? A man maybe?

The receptionist shakes her head.

Kate   I'd like to take that room, please.

She enters Room 12. She senses **Alexei***'s presence. Pause.*

But then her tinnitus returns. She takes out her laptop and Skypes.

In London **Michael** *answers.*

Michael   Hi. How's Moscow?

Kate   I've just arrived?

Michael   How are the Finns?

Kate   The Finns?

Michael   Aren't Nokia Finnish?

Kate   I'm meeting them in an hour.

Michael   Give them hell. I'm heading over to Peter's studio. Some reel-to-reels from 1990 have arrived. Listen, about what I said, I really mea . . . really miss . . .

The Skype is freezing.

I was just . . . what you said earlier . . . can you . . . b . . . can I . . . ev . . . Mn . . . several . . .

Kate   Michael, I'm losing you. Michael?

Michael   . . . love . . . can . . . b . . .

Kate   Michael I'm losing you, you're breaking up. I'm going to email. I'm going to email.

And she starts to email . . .

But then the sound of manual typing enters her mind and a memory overtakes her . . .

Scene Five

THE TRAVEL BUREAU

Moscow ex-Soviet travel department, 1991.

Nikolas *introduces the Travel Bureau, an old abandoned warehouse in Moscow.*

Nikolas   In 1956 Nikita Khrushchev takes the podium on the last day of the Communist Party Congress and does the unthinkable, denouncing his predecessor, Josef Stalin, as a tyrant who'd done little but to have hundreds of thousands to their deaths or to the gulags.

Krushchev's Soviet Union will be different, he says. We will send comrades to the seaside, to the forests and the mountains. To, from and across the whole of the Eastern Bloc.

And this is where it all happened. 1956. One girl, one typewriter. And by 1959 the Department for Inter-Soviet Travel was employing close to three hundred people. Sending comrades on holiday from Kiev to Riga, from Moscow to Prague.

Girls over here handle orders. A phone rings. Some comrade wants to visit Tbilisi. Budgets are agreed. Duplicate copies to the clerks who process each request. And, where possible, give the successful applicants the three-week break needed to help lubricate the Soviet state's insatiable appetite for compliance.

It closed when the wall came down. And now it's just another empty warehouse Until tonight.

Because tonight, we turn this place into the Travel Bureau.

Dance music playing. **Alexei** *and* **Nikolas** *are working on the space, preparing for opening night.* **Kate** *is watching.*

Alexei   What do you think?

Kate   This is going to be the club?

Alexei   This is the club.

Kate   There's nothing here.

Nikolas   Exactly, that's the whole point

Alexei   Every Russian idea has come from above. Orthodox religion told us how to be good.

Nikolas   Communism ordered us to be equal.

Alexei   None of it the people owned. None of it we felt.

Nikolas   Whatever the Travel Bureau becomes, it will be what people make it.

Alexei   Why did you go to Berlin?

Kate   I love the scene.

Alexei   But why Berlin?

Kate   Freedom!

Alexei   We drove two thousand miles in a car –

Nikolas   – stinking of fish –

Alexei   – to smell that freedom. We want that here. Now.

Kate   How do you know they'll come?

He lights a cigarette. A young girl enters and helps **Nikolas** *spray the wall:* **Irina**.

Nikolas   How many people are there in Russia?

Kate   No idea

Alexei   Here one hundred and forty million.

Nikolas   Of those, forty million are under twenty-five. Moscow State University has thirty thousand students.

Alexei   Walk down the street, you'll fall over a hundred teenagers drinking moonshine, smoking whatever they can get their hands on. They have nothing and they don't even realise, think to complain.

Nikolas   Because no one has taught them to question what they're missing.

Alexei   That's why when we stuck a thousand messages on lamp posts all over the Moscow University State Campus, the opening night of the Travel Bureau sold out in two hours.

Kate   Tonight?

Alexei   But it'll last three nights. Four nights. A week. That's what this is about.

The tape they are listening to suddenly gets caught in the machine. **Nikolas** *takes it out. Long strands of tape. He throws it to* **Alexei**, *who starts to fix it. He stares at the tape.*

Nikolas   Ah man!

Alexei   Irina. Pass me that pencil.

Irina *passes him the pencil.*

Kate   Who's Irina?

Alexei   My god-daughter. You have that in England?

Kate   We have that.

Alexei   She is from my home town.

Kate   Is that all she is?

Alexei   She's fifteen.

Kate   Why is she in Moscow?

Alexei   She's come to say goodbye.

Kate   Where is she going?

Alexei   She's not. I am.

Pause. He winds the tape. Stares at it. **Nikolas** *sprays the wall as the scene continues quietly between* **Alexei** *and* **Kate**.

Alexei   When did you first listen to the Rolling Stones?

Kate   My home in Southampton. My sister and I could hear 'Gimme Shelter' coming from my parents' bedroom. It always meant the same thing – no entry for two hours.

Alexei   Our home town is a thousand miles south of Moscow. Forest to the east, the river to the west. Every month Nikolas received a parcel in the post. Inside was a C90 audio tape, just like this. The tape was from Nikolai's cousin . . .

Nikolas   He's my uncle . . .

Alexei   Uncle . . . in Moscow.

Nikolas   Who had a friend in Leningrad . . .

Alexei   As it was then.

Nikolas   Who knew an Estonian who could smuggle music into the country.

Alexei   Western music.

Nikolas   Illegal music.

Alexei   Rolling Stones. Little Richard.

Nikolas   Motown.

Alexei   Screaming Jay Hawkins.

Nikolas   And then, later, dance music . . .

Alexei   And this music was sent secretly from person to person across the country, copied, again and again, until you could barely hear it on the tape. My sister Natasha was three years older than me. We'd go out into the forest with the tapes.

Nikolas   And a Samsung Midi imported from Iran . . .

Alexei   And press 'play'. Under the pine trees.

Club receding now. Slight isolation now for **Alexei** *and* **Kate**.

Alexei   Somewhere where no one could hear us. Once we stayed there all night listening to Ray Charles. She climbed the pines in her grey dress and danced on the branches for hours. Like a teenage banshee. I'd lie on the ground and watch her. Never seen someone so free . . .

He stares at **Kate**. *She understands. She is closer.*

Light changes. Scene begins to shift.

Alexei   What are you most afraid of?

Kate   Deafness. I am afraid of losing my hearing.

Pause. Very close.

Alexei   If you could be anywhere right now, where would you be?

Kate   Here.

Scene Six

MOSCOW HOTEL ROOM — KATE AND ALEXEI I

A few days later. Moscow hotel, Room 12, 1991.

Kate *and* **Alexei**. *They have been in there for five days. She has missed three flights. They are madly in love.*

He plays a song on the tape machine. They lie close.

Alexei   How many flights have you missed?

Kate   Seven.

They kiss.

Where is your sister now?

Alexei   She married a factory worker.

Kate   Is she happy?

Alexei   She grows potatoes.

Kiss.

Kate   When do you have to leave?

Alexei   I have to be at the recruitment office in one hour.

Kate   Don't go.

Alexei   You want me to go jail? I have avoided it for three years.

Kate   How did they find you?

Alexei   Spot check at a metro station in the east of the city. Had my name on a list. They wanted to take me straight away, but Nikolai's money bought me two weeks. Two weeks is up.

Kate   Nikolas got out of it?

Alexei   Nikolas has a rich uncle.

Kate   I'm rich.

Alexei (*joking*)   I don't want your dirty western money.

She laughs. Then serious.

Kate   What's it gonna be like?

He does not answer.

Alexei   I'll write every week.

Kate   Every day.

Alexei   Every day.

They kiss. He starts to dress. Long pause. She draws him. He stands to leave.

Alexei   Same room, same time, next year.

And back in 2010 **Kate** *remembers as* **Michael** *tries to Skype.*

Scene Seven

600 HOURS OF TAPE

London, 2010.

Michael *Skyping, failing to get through.*

Peter *listening to 600 hours of BBC tapes. Nothing apparently on them. Boredom.*

Voice on Tape   June 2nd, end of reel G, 9051.

Michael, *who is holding a pad and pencil, is on the telephone.*

Michael   Once again I'm really sorry, Mrs Smith, my condolences on the loss of your husband. No, it's a, um, a documentary for Channel 4 on the Met. Your husband's name should have been taken off that list. I apologise. Thank you very much. All the best.

Peter *is changing the reel-to-reel during this.*

Michael   Dead. Deceased.

Don't laugh.

That's the third one now. Mr Smith is no more.

Jesus, I have four hundred police officers from the 1980s on this list . . . How am I . . .

Peter *puts headphones on. Audience hears reel-to-reel voice-over.*

Voice on Tape   June 2nd, end of reel H, 9051.

Peter   Same voice . . .

Michael Do you know what pisses me off? Sarah fucking Whitfield doesn't have to do this. She has a team behind her. You worked for her, didn't you? The 'real hurt locker'; give me a break.

Telephone rings.

Peter *changes tape reel.*

Michael Steven, hi! Yes, No it's going amazingly right now. We've got some real gold. Some real gold dust. Yeah. No, no, no, no, no. You're gonna have to give us a couple more days on this, because, well, basically there's over 600 hours of tape. I'm not sure we're gonna be able to deliver on Wednesday. I'll have the taster tape by Friday.

On the tape we hear:

Voice on Tape June 4th, end of reel K, 9051. DI Barber.

Peter *rewinds.*

Voice on Tape DI Barber.

Peter Listen to this.

Michael *listens. His face lights up.*

Michael Barber, there's a Barber on the list.

Scene Eight

TRYING TO CONTACT KENNETH BARBER

Michael *and a* **BBC Producer** *calling* **Kenneth Barber** *again and again, desperately trying to get through to him. In his house in Lewisham* **Kenneth** *stares at the phone.*

Michael Kenneth Barber? It's Michael Bellerose from the BBC. Sorry to keep calling. I just wanted to chat to you about the film I'm making – can you get back to me? Once again my number is 07930 . . .

The phone rings again and again. At last **Kenneth** *picks it up.*

Kenneth Hello? Kenneth Barber speaking.

Scene Nine

MOSCOW HOTEL ROOM — KATE AND ALEXEI 2

Moscow, the hotel room, 1992. **Kate** *and* **Alexei**. *He plays the same music as in the previous hotel scene. Pause as she draws him.*

Kate   What's wrong?

Alexei   They said they were going to keep us on. For another year.

Kate   Can they do that?

Alexei   They can do whatever they want.

Kate   Why?

Alexei   They want to fight a war. In the south. They need men.

Kate   How did you get out of it?

Alexei *smiles.*

Alexei   I escaped.

Kate   You did what?

Alexei   I climbed the fence out of the base. Walked for seven hours to a train station. Hid amongst the grain sacks.

Kate   What if they find you?

Alexei   They won't.

Kate   How do you know?

Alexei   Because I'll be in England.

Kate   England?

Alexei   There's nothing for me here.

Pause. Music.

Marry me.

Kate   What?

Alexei   Marry me.

Pause.

Kate   Why did you stop writing?

Alexei   I told you. I didn't.

Pause.

There's something you're not telling me.

Pause.

Have you met someone else?

Kate   Of course not.

Pause.

Alexei   Have you met someone else?

Pause.

Kate   You stopped writing.

Alexei   I did not stop writing! I wrote a letter every week . . .

Kate   Well, I didn't get them!

Pause.

Alexei   What's his name?

Kate   His name's not important.

Alexei   What's his name?

Kate   It didn't mean anything. I was lonely. I hadn't heard from you for six months. It was nothing!

Pause.

Dance with me.

They dance. He grabs her. Hard. Very hard.

Let me go.

Pause. He lets go. Takes the tape machine. Walks out of the room.

Dissolve back to 2010. **Kate** *wondering what her next move should be. Her tinnitus is bad. She calls on the hotel phone.*

Kate   Hi. I'm looking for the number of the Travel Bureau. It's a club outside Moscow?

Voice   The Travel Bureau does not exist any more.

Kate   I'm looking for a man called Nikolas Borbaky.

Voice   Nikolas Borbaky? The businessman?

Kate   Yes. I think so. Do you know him?

Voice (*sigh*)   Please hold.

Muzak. She is on hold.

Yes, I have a number for Mr Borbaky's offices.

Scene Ten

PETER AND MARY 2

Morning. **Peter** *in his apartment. Listening to his neighbour* **Mary**. *The same routine at first.*

She enters. Creaking floorboards. Sounds of crockery and cutlery, her opening the fridge.

Then the phone rings.

Mary   Shit. Shit.

She rejects the call. It rings again. She clearly recognises the number.

OK. OK.

She answers. **Peter** *is listening.*

Mary   Why are you calling? . . . It's seven in the morning. What time is it there?

Are you drunk?

Look, this is . . . really hard for me. I love . . .

The sound of an aeroplane covers the words.

. . . really hurt me. Do you know that? Yes, but you do it every time.

Sound of tap on. Water. Tap off.

. . . a piss? I'm just washing my hands. (*Laughs.*) Washing hands.

No, I can't just jump on a plane . . .

Toaster noise. Toast in.

No. Absolutely no way.

It's taken me a year getting my life back together.

I have a job, I have my own flat.

Do you realise what happened to me?

Do you have any idea?

I said NO . . .

She hangs up.

Fucking . . .

Scene dissolves . . .

Scene Eleven

LEWISHAM CAFE/MOSCOW RESTAURANT

Michael *arrives in a café in Lewisham.*

Michael (*to waitress*)   Cup of coffee, please. Do you do latte? OK, just coffee then.

Kate *arrives in a very swish Moscow hotel.*

Kate (*to waiter*)   Table booked for Mr Borbaky?

A glass of freshly squeezed orange juice, please.

In Lewisham **Kenneth** *enters.* **Kenneth** *sees* **Michael.**

Kenneth   Michael Bellerose?

Michael   Kenneth.

In Moscow, **Nikolas** *sees* **Kate**.

Nikolas (*to waiter*)   Two Dirty Martinis, please. I'm sorry. I'm late.

Kate   Only an hour.

Nikolas   God. You haven't changed a bit.

Kate   Neither have you. You're still a liar.

In Lewisham.

Michael   Thanks for meeting me.

Kenneth   I didn't have much choice. Where did you get that recording?

Michael   It's publicly available. We just bothered to listen to the six hundred hours of birdsong that came before it. Can I get you a coffee?

In Moscow.

Kate   Thanks for meeting me. You're a busy man.

Nikolas   Always time for old friends. You look great.

Kate   So do you.

Nikolas   Yeah, I'm doing OK.

Kate   Sounds like it. It took me twenty minutes to get through your various receptionists. Whatever happened to the Travel Bureau?

Nikolas   I sold it a long time ago. Along with a couple of other clubs. They changed the name, but it's still there.

Kate   What's it called now?

Nikolas   I can't remember.

Kate   What's it like?

Nikolas   I don't know. Honestly. I don't go there. You haven't done badly yourself . . .

Kate   Yeah, I've done OK.

Nikolas (*to waiter*)   Can I have two menus please?

He takes her hand.

Oh, hello. Married woman.

Kate   Yup.

Nikolas   So who is the lucky man?

In Lewisham.

Michael   I haven't been in Lewisham for a few years. My sister had her child in the Lewisham Hospital, very good post-natal care, which I remember surprised us at the time . . .

And as **Michael** *continues his chatter, we fade to Moscow.*

Nikolas   Children?

Kate   No. You?

Nikolas   Children – several.

Kate   Married?

Nikolas   For now. So who do you work for?

Kate   Galleon. Sponsorship agency.

Nikolas   You're here on business?

Kate   No.

Nikolas   Pleasure.

Kate   This came. In the post.

She brings out the tape.

Nikolas   Let me guess. Bill Haley.

Kate   Little Richard. Do you know where he is?

Nikolas   Little Richard?

Kate   Alexei Skorik.

Nikolas   Last time I saw Alex was seven years ago.

Kate   What happened?

Nikolas   We had a difference of opinion.

Kate   But you guys were so close.

Nikolas   Isn't life strange?

Kate   What happened?

Smash cut to the Travel Bureau club. Seven years ago.

Alexei   Look at me in the eyes and tell me what you've done.

Nikolas   From the beginning? Well I worked twenty hours a day, seven days a week, I built bars, wrote leaflets, paid off gangsters – where were you?

Alexei   I was in hospital.

Nikolas   In some luxury hotel on the Baltic . . .

Alexei   I was in a military hospital . . .

Nikolas   Remind me. What injury did you fake?

Alexei   It took us six years to make this place. What did we say? The people always decide.

Nikolas   Well, you know what?

Alexei   The people!

Nikolas   The people decided . . .

Alexei   Not the small number who can afford your highly expensive membership prices.

Nikolas   The people decided that what they wanted was somewhere private and comfortable they could sit down in, have a drink, not be assaulted or glassed . . .

Alexei   Look at this. Three levels of membership! Platinum, gold and silver.

Nikolas   It makes them feel better about themselves!

Alexei   Who are those guys at the door?

Nikolas   Do you want a platinum membership?

Alexei   Who are you in business with?

Pause.

Who are you in business with?

Nikolas   The guys on the door are security.

Alexei   They wouldn't let me in my own club!

Nikolas   They didn't know who you were! You pitch up out of nowhere, no phone call . . .

Alexei   Get them out of here.

Nikolas   I don't think so.

Alexei   Get them out of here now!

Nikolas   The world has changed . . .

Alexei   If you won't, I will.

Nikolas   What medication are you on?

Beat.

Alexei   What did you say?

Nikolas   What medication are you on?

Alexei   I'll break your fucking legs.

Nikolas   Do I have to call security? Do I?

Pause. **Alexei** *leaves. Back in 2010 in Moscow.*

Nikolas   It was no big deal.

Kate   Where did he go?

Nikolas   I honestly don't know. I thought he might try to find you.

Pause.

Kate   No. He never did.

Nikolas   His brain wasn't the same when he came back. You know that.

Kate   Do I?

Nikolas   It's in the past. Leave it there.

Pause.

Listen, how long are you in town? I have a house outside Moscow, original style, there's a banya, chickens, and the view of the hills is really beautiful. I can cancel my arrangements for the weekend, we could go out there, relive old times . . .

Pause.

Kate   I want to find him.

Pause.

Nikolas   Something missing at home?

Kate   None of your business.

Nikolas   Well then, if I were you, I'd go and see the Kremlin, queue up for Lenin's corpse, and then go home. (*To waiter.*) Put this on my tab. (*To* **Kate**.) There's nothing for you here.

In Lewisham.

Michael   – so they put the cycling lanes in and it makes it so much easier. Another coffee?

Kenneth   Why are we here?

Michael   OK. Let me tell you what I'd like to do. I'd like to come to your house, it makes it easier for you, and then we'll just chat. I'm not out to get you . . . I just want to get your side of the story, as much as you feel comfortable talking about, and no more . . .

Michael *tells* **Kenneth** *it will all be fine, talks him through it. As he does so the tables part, the waitress turns into a make-up woman,* **Peter** *does the mike through the jacket, the camera appears magically as if from nowhere and we are right bang in the middle of shooting in* **Kenneth***'s living room.*

Scene Twelve

KENNETH AND MICHAEL INTERVIEW I

Kenneth*'s house, Lewisham, 2010.* **Michael, Kenneth, Peter.** *Camera.* **Peter** *with mike and headphones.*

Kenneth   The Poll Tax riots took us all by surprise. Bricks being hurled in Trafalgar Square. Kids in black balaclavas thinking they were anarchists. We had no intelligence, no surveillance, nothing. You had the GLC stirring it up. Militant groups turning student demos into all-out chaos. We were losing control.

In April 1990 I was approached by a senior officer in the Met about a new unit. Unit 51.

Michael   Can you remember the name of the officer?

Kenneth   The unit was to be a surveillance and infiltration operation. Bit like the old ghost squads of the 60s. Except this was different. This was to be taken out of the direct control of the Met, almost like private security, still reporting to Special Branch but basically hands-off.

Michael   Unaccountable.

Kenneth   We were all given a basic training in surveillance, bugs, wire taps, standard tradecraft. Then we were given a list of suspects, individuals who people upstairs thought might be influential in the militant movement.

Michael   OK, so let's say I'm on that list, what would you do?

Kenneth   We'd normally bug the house first.

Michael   How would you do that?

Kenneth   I might be a gasman, landlord's agents, cleaners, anything to get inside. Then once that was done, most of the time was spent in a van a few hundred yards down the road, drinking coffee and listening.

Michael   What did you hear?

Kenneth   Mostly I heard people watching TV, arguing and having sex. That's what they seem to do most in my experience.

Michael   Something exciting must have happened.

Kenneth   Every now and then we changed the colour of the van.

He is blocking.

Michael   Who was on that list? Anyone I'd know?

Kenneth   I don't recall.

Pause.

Michael   Who's the girl in the photographs? On the stairs?

Kenneth   That's my daughter. Cassie.

Michael   Your only daughter?

Pause. **Kenneth** *nods.*

Michael   She's pretty. How old is she now?

Kenneth   Thirty-one. Yeah.

Michael   She's not thirty-one in the photos.

Pause.

Kenneth   I haven't seen her in a while.

Michael   Why's that?

Kenneth   My wife and I separated. She took my wife's part. It happens.

Peter *walks away. Intention to relax the atmosphere. Kettle on.*

Michael   I'm hoping to have children myself.

Kenneth   You should get a move on.

Michael   I'm planning to. Work kind of gets in the way.

Kenneth   Don't let it. You married?

Michael   Five years.

Kenneth   Then what you waiting for?

Michael   Where is Cassie now?

Pause.

Kenneth   I don't know.

Michael   When did you last see her?

Kenneth   Fif . . . fifteen years ago.

Pause.

Michael   Who was on the list, Kenneth?

Michael *leaves the scene, which continues on a TV screen and with*
Kenneth *staying live. He is now in the editing suite. BBC producers on*
conference call. **Michael** *and* **Peter** *in the suite.*

BBC Producer   Sophie and I are in TV Centre.

Michael   OK, I'm streaming this to you now.

Kenneth   Just all the usual suspects. GLC. Red Wedgies.

Sophie   Listen, Michael, you're already a month late with
this.

Kenneth   Trying to turn CND demos into class war.

Michael   Just listen please. This is Kenneth Barber. Ex-
surveillance of the Met. I have him on camera admitting he
was a member of Unit 51. (*On screeen.*) There must be some
names . . . some names you can remember . . . (*In the suite.*)
But there's more than that. There's something he isn't telling
me.

Kenneth   I don't remember.

Michael   Look. Look. He's lying.

BBC Producer   So what are you asking for?

Michael   I need three more days . . . I need Peter to be paid . . .

Sophie   You've said this before. I'm just not sure there's anything here.

Pause. **Michael** *presses 'pause'.*

Michael   Please. I'm telling you. There's something he isn't telling me.

Scene Thirteen

KATE ON THE PHONE TO MICHAEL

Moscow/London 2010.

Kate *walking to the station. She is calling an excited* **Michael** *who is thrilled at his coup with* **Kenneth**.

Kate   Michael?

Michael   Hi! How are you?

Kate   I'm OK. Listen . . .

Michael   OK, listen to this. You know I got that call from Peter? OK, so we went through the tapes right, and there was this name. Kenneth Barber. A copper. So I called him and we met and . . . what does he only go and say, on camera? He's a member of Unit 51. He's not telling me everything but he knows something. I'm sure of it. This could be the breakthrough we've been waiting for.

Kate   I'm not here because of Nokia.

Pause.

Michael   What?

Kate   That's not why I'm here.

Michael   I don't understand. Why are you there?

Kate   I'm about to catch a train.

Michael   A train where?

Kate   South. Eight hundred miles. I'm not coming back tomorrow. I've told work . . .

Michael   Work! What the hell are you doing?

Kate   I got a letter. In the post. It was from Alexei. Alexei Skorik? You remember I told you about him, my friend from Russia?

Michael   Why didn't you tell me this before?

Kate   Because I didn't want to upset you.

Michael   Listen, just come home!

Kate   I think he's in trouble . . . I have to find out if he's OK. I'll just be a few more days, I thought he was in Moscow but he's not.

Michael   Just come home, Kate.

Kate   I'm going to go to his home town, it's in the south, on the Volga. I'll call you when I get there. Michael, tell me you understand. Michael . . .

But **Michael** *is thinking about a dinner party in 2005 . . .*

Scene Fourteen

DINNER PARTY

London, 2005. Dinner party. The Post-it note game. **Michael** *and* **Kate***'s flat – the happy couple amidst friends.*

Michael   OK, am I a man? Am I alive? Am I in a position of immense power? Am I renowned documentarian Michael Bellerose?

And then suddenly there is a ringing at the front door.

Michael *goes to answer the door. It is* **Alexei***.*

Michael   Hi.

Alexei   Hi sorry to be . . . My English is not good. Is Kate in?

Michael   Sorry, you are . . . ?

Alexei   Alex. Alexei Skorik. I am an old friend of Kate's.

Michael   Oh yes. Yes, Kate told me about you.

Alexei   Is she here?

Michael   She's away on business. I've got a few close friends around, we're watching the football. Would you like to join us?

Alexei   No. When is she coming back?

Michael   Tomorrow. How long are you in town?

Alexei   Until Monday.

Michael   Well, I'll tell her you called.

Alexei   Sorry. You are . . .

Michael   I'm her husband. Listen, I should probably be getting back in . . .

Pause. **Alexei** *produces a parcel.*

Alexei   Please would you give her this. Please. Just tell her I called and give her this.

Michael   Of course. Is there a number she can get you on?

Alexei   Just give her this.

Michael   Sure. Hey. Nice to meet you.

Alexei *leaves.* **Michael** *opens the parcel and finds letters inside. He looks at them, then puts them in his pocket.*

Kate   Who was that at the door?

Michael   Just Dean from across the road. They're going away for a week, want us to water their herbs. That's hippies for you.

Kate   They're not hippies.

Michael   They're on the way.

Kate   Tonight was wonderful.

They kiss.

Michael   Was it? I know it was mainly my friends.

She stops his mouth.

Kate   Come to bed.

Scene Fifteen

RUSSIAN TRAIN JOURNEY

Russian train, 2010.

Kate *heads south. Different people occupy the seat opposite as around her the landscape is transformed.*

Scene Sixteen

PETER AND MARY 3

Hounslow, 2010. Night.

Peter *listening to* **Mary***, who enters drunk. She breaks crockery, stumbles, turns on water, leaves it on, opens fridge. Her phone rings.*

Mary   Caroline? Yeah, I'm OK . . . I shouldn't have gone. I knew I shouldn't. Did I make a fool of myself? Are you sure?

No, I won't call him. I won't I promise . . . I won't! My laptop's at work! How can I email him when my laptop's sitting in Terminal 2?

OK. OK.

She hangs up. Starts to cry.

Peter *breaks a life's rule and walks into her apartment as she has left the door open.*

He stares at her but says nothing. He just can't.

He leaves.

He then hears as **Mary** *takes something from her bag, and starts to type.*

Scene Seventeen

PETER AND KENNETH WAIT FOR MICHAEL

Kenneth's *house.* **Peter** *and* **Kenneth** *wait for* **Michael**, *who is late. Peter has a mug of tea.*

Kenneth   Do you want a biscuit with that?

Peter   I'm all right, thanks.

Kenneth   He's delayed, I expect.

I'm thinking I should put on a fresh shirt.

Kenneth *changes his shirt.* **Peter** *sees his moon tattoo.*

Peter   The tattoo on your arm.

Kenneth   It's a Chinese character. For moon. I was persuaded by my daughter. There was this album called *Yellow Moon* by the Neville Brothers. To wind me up I remember her saying, 'Dad, you should get a yellow moon tattooed over your heart.' So I did.

Peter   I always wanted to walk on the moon. Just to hear what it was like.

Kenneth   I listened to the landings on the radio. Buzz Aldrin, Neil Armstrong. Hearing those voices, it was like another world. Like the universe just got smaller. We were capable of anything.

Peter's *phone rings.*

Peter   That's him now.

Kenneth   Can I trust him?

Pause.

Peter   Sure.

Kenneth   OK. Tell him I'd like to talk. About James Hansford.

Peter *stares at* **Kenneth**. *Pause. Then he answers call.* **Michael** *is on the phone.*

Michael   Peter, listen, I think I need to go away for a couple of days.

Peter   OK.

Michael   Apologise to him. I just have to go to Russia, just for two days.

Peter   He says he wants to talk. About James Hansford.

Pause.

Michael   When did he say that?

Peter   Just now.

Michael   You sure he said James Hansford?

Peter   What do you want me to do?

Pause.

Michael   Nothing. I'm coming over. I'll be there in half an hour.

Scene Eighteen

KATE AT NATASHA AND IVAN'S HOUSE

Kate *at* **Alexei**'s *family house in a small town on the Volga, with* **Natasha** *and* **Ivan**. *They sit at a table watching Russian TV.*

Natasha   It will dry in no time.

Kate   Thanks.

Natasha   It's a long journey. And then just as you arrive. The rain.

Kate   This is kind.

Ivan   Where are your bags?

Kate   I left them at the hotel.

Natasha   She left them at the hotel. It's a nice hotel, isn't it?

Ivan   It's the only hotel.

Natasha   Well, he'll be back in a minute.

Kate   And he's all right?

Natasha   He told us all about you.

Kate   Did he?

Natasha   He's been living here ever since he came back.

Kate   Why did he come back?

Natasha   This is his home.

Kate   Is he married?

Natasha   Oh no. Are you?

Kate   Yes.

Natasha   That's nice. It's nice to be married. We're married. Get her some soup. Children?

Kate   Not yet. We're thinking about it.

Natasha   Don't leave it too late.

Kate   Where is he?

Natasha   He just popped out. Should be any time now. You live in London?

Kate   Yes.

Natasha   That's nice.

Kate   He told me about you. You used to dance together.

Pause. **Ivan** *brings the soup.*

Natasha   Here's the soup.

Kate   Thank you.

Ivan   Don't eat the foot. It's for taste.

Natasha   Did you put salt in it?

Ivan   I put salt.

Natasha   He forgets the salt.

Kate   Do you have any photographs?

She gets up.

Any photographs of him?

Natasha   We do somewhere. Ivan, we must somewhere.

Pause.

Kate   Will he be back soon?

Natasha   Of course he will. This is his home.

And suddenly **Alexei** *is in the house, some time earlier, unhappy after returning from London, hating his life, hating the house . . . His sister dances with* **Ivan** *to music on the radio.*

Alexei *turns on the TV to drown the music. A war film. Gunfire.* **Ivan** *turns off the radio.*

Ivan *sits next to* **Alexei***. He turns off the TV. Pause.*

Alexei *turns on the TV, loud.*

Ivan *turns over the TV to another quieter, sweeter channel.*

Alexei *turns it back.*

Ivan *turns it back.*

Natasha *enters and watches.*

Alexei *turns it back.*

Ivan *turns it off.*

Alexei *turns it back on.*

Ivan *tries to turn it off but* **Alexei** *grabs his arm. Stillness.* **Alexei** *forces* **Ivan***'s hand away from the TV.*

Pause.

Alexei *stands, war film still on loud, and tries to force* **Natasha** *to dance. But then he stops, suddenly broken, almost weeping. Stillness.*

Then he gets his coat and heads out of the house.

Back in the present. **Ivan** *stares at* **Kate**.

Ivan   He's never coming back.

Scene Nineteen

KENNETH AND MICHAEL INTERVIEW 2

Kenneth*'s house.*

Kenneth   James Hansford lived in Brockley, just off the Lewisham Road. He was twenty-eight years old. Ever since he'd studied up in Liverpool he'd been involved in all the militant movements. We'd had eyes on him for a while.

What kicked it off was a student demo at South London Poly.

We broke it up, but one policeman got a bit enthusiastic with a baton and cracked this young girl's skull. Hansford took advantage of that, he got on the news, on the radio, alleging this, alleging that, all nonsense, . . .

Michael   So someone decided to take him down.

Kenneth   We were told that if we could find anything, anything, criminal, or dodgy, anything at all, on Hansford, that would be job done. They wanted him to be dodging tax, or sleeping with girls he was teaching . . .

Michael   What were they going to do with that information?

Kenneth   You'd have to ask them that.

Michael   So you bugged his flat.

Kenneth   I listened to him for six months. Every bloody day.

Michael   And?

Kenneth   Nothing. He was smart, he didn't talk about anything on the phone, he never met anyone in the house. It was like he knew.

Michael   So you got nothing.

Kenneth   Nothing.

Pause.

Michael   James Hansford was killed on the night of 29 October 1990. Were you still operating surveillance on him at that time?

Pause. **Kenneth** *nods.*

Michael   Were you in the van that day?

Pause.

Did you hear anything?

Pause.

Hansford was found with a wound to his leg, and his chest. There was broken glass. You must have heard something.

Kenneth   It happened in the night. We'd clocked off.

Michael   I don't believe you.

Pause.

Why did you agree to meet me? You didn't need to, you could have stayed silent as you have for twenty years. Why did you let me into your house?

Pause.

I think you want to talk to me.

Pause.

Kenneth   The day of 29 October I was in the van.
Hansford was on the phone a great deal. It was a Saturday.
He wasn't at work.

Pause.

There was football on the radio. It was still the old First
Division then. Hansford was an Everton fan. He was listening
to Everton Villa.

He turned up the volume of the football. Louder than
normal. Louder than necessary. He was on the phone, but
I couldn't hear it.

He didn't want me to hear it. Or his neighbour. Or someone.

He was talking to someone on the phone. And after six
months of listening in to Going for Fucking Gold, we couldn't
hear a word.

Pause.

So I decided to stay for the night.

Michael   Just you?

Kenneth   Yeah. Just me.

Pause.

Michael   All night?

Kenneth   All night.

Pause.

Kenneth   Can I have a moment?

Michael   Why'd you need a moment?

Peter   Just give him a moment.

Kenneth *leaves. He's left his radio mike on.* **Peter** *hears the sounds
of* **Kenneth** *suppressing panic, even tears, in the next-door room.*
Peter *looks at* **Michael,** *who is unaware of this and is on the phone,
laughing to a TV producer.* **Peter** *takes off the headphones.*

Michael   I've got him, Steven. Listen, can you get a viewing room booked in TV Centre for Monday. I want to show this and then I need to head out to Russia. Yeah, it's gold dust. Yeah. Oh yeah.

Scene Twenty

KATE AND JOSEF

Kate *in a dingy hotel room in a town on the Volga. Going a bit crazy.*

She tries to sleep, can't, gets up.

Walks through the hotel corridor sequence. Rooms, sounds of rooms.

Then suddenly she meets **Josef***, the nightwatchman.*

Kate   Aaaagh!

Josef   It's OK. I work here. You awake?

Kate   I need some water.

Josef   Come. Come.

He takes her to the front desk and gives her water.

You stay here alone.

She nods.

Josef   Long way from home.

She is crying. He approaches her, holds her gently.

There now. You are lonely. Yes? It can be lonely. I am happy on my own . . . I am forest guard. Me and one other man. There is nothing. Just us and the wolves. But some people don't like it . . .

Her phone goes.

Kate   Michael.

Michael   Listen, where are you? I've been calling, no reception . . .

Kate   Michael, I'm coming home.

Pause.

I'm coming home.

Michael   When?

Kate   Tomorrow morning. I'll book it now.

Michael   I'm sorry I lost it.

Kate   No, I'm sorry . . .

Michael   Just come home. OK? We'll talk, we'll talk about everything.

Kate   I love you.

Michael   I love you.

She hangs up. Pause. She shivers.

Josef   You are cold.

Kate   I need a phone number, please. The nearest airport. Customer information.

He is fetching her a coat. He puts it round her. Big green coat.

Josef   Keep you warm. I will find number.

She smells the coat. Sudden change.

Kate   Where did you get this? Is this yours?

Josef   It belongs to the other forest guard. I took it by mistake when I left yesterday. Now he has mine. He is much bigger than me.

He laughs.

Kate   Where is he?

Josef   Where is the hut?

Kate   Yes, where is it?

Josef   Not far outside town, on the road east. You take a right down a track between the pines. It's narrow. At the fork you take a right, left takes you back to the lake. The lodge is not far down the track. You'll find him there.

Scene Twenty-One

KENNETH AND MICHAEL INTERVIEW 3

Kenneth's *house.* **Michael** *and* **Kenneth.** **Peter** *listening on headphones.*

Kenneth   It was nine o'clock when he decided to go out. He called this girl, he had a few girls, quite a hit with the birds he was. They arranged to meet at the Old Bull down on Lewisham High Street and then they were going to spend the night at hers. I heard him packing a few things. Toiletries.

Pause.

Then he headed out of the door of his flat. You have to understand. I'd heard him leave that flat a hundred times. And there was something about the way the door sounded. The click of the door as it closed behind him. That evening it didn't. He hadn't shut the door. Maybe he was thinking about his bird. But he didn't take care.

Then he left the building.

Michael   For the night.

Kenneth   I waited an hour. Just to be sure. Then I got out of the van, went up to the house. It was one of those big Victorian semis with about seven buzzers next to the door. I pressed all of them until someone let me in. No questions asked. I went up to the third floor. I was right. Door was settled on the latch.

Inside. I knew the layout before I even walked in. I'd listened to him for so bloody long I could have lived there myself. I'd even guessed the colours of the walls. I knew where the phone was. I even knew he had a pad of paper in between the phone and the fridge.

It had everything on it we needed. It was a plan for the next demo. They were going to disguise militants as students and smuggle them into this demo in Manchester. I had names, phone numbers. I had what I'd been waiting for.

That's when he came back.

Michael James Hansford?

Kenneth I don't know why. Maybe he'd forgotten his condoms. He walked in and saw me. He went straight for the phone. I couldn't let him call. I got between him and the phone. He tried to grab me, started to shout at me. I tried to push him away, tried to get to the door, just to get out of there. But he wouldn't let me out. He was incensed. He got me by the neck, tried to drag me across into the living room. I kicked him hard in the shins, and then I punched him. I thought I'd got away, I reached the door but he came back at me, and I turned and . . .

There was this paper knife on the little beech shelf by the door. It was instinct. I grabbed it, just waved it at him, it was a pathetic looking thing and he laughed and came at me and I just held it out and he ran at me and it just . . .

It went in. There was red on his shirt. It was a nice shirt, he'd dressed up for the bird. He looked at me, a bit sort of surprised . . .

He sank down. Looked at me. His mouth opened. 'Call someone. Call someone.'

I walked past him. Pulled the phone out.

And I walked out.

I left him.

Michael and **Peter** *in the editing suite, watching this confession.*

Michael Get the sound done tonight. I want to show this tomorrow.

Peter *left alone.*

Scene Twenty-Two

MARY HAS GONE

Peter *returns home to find* **Mary** *gone.*

Scene Twenty-Three

FOREST LODGE I

Forest lodge outside Russian town, 2010. The sound of a car approaching on a muddy track. A door slams and the car goes back the way it came.

Kate *enters the lodge with torch. She sees* **Alexei's** *boots. Recognises them. She sees the old tape recorder, puts the tape in and the rock'n'roll music plays. 'Rip It Up'. A moment of memory.*

But then **Kate** *sees a woman's hat in the hut. A hat she recognises.* **Irina***'s hat.*

Kate *hears a car approaching. A door slams.*

Kate *tense with expectation.*

Enter **Irina**. *Pause.*

Kate   Who are you?

Irina   I didn't think you'd come.

Kate   What do you mean?

Irina   Don't you recognise me?

She puts the hat on.

Kate   The god-daughter. In the club. You look different.

Irina   I was younger then. We all were.

Did you know that Stalin buried thousands of dissidents in this forest? We've managed to find some of the burial grounds, deep in the woods. But many others must still remain. And when you do dig them up, it's almost impossible to identify the bones.

Kate   Where is Alex?

Irina *lights a cigarette.*

Kate   How did you know he sent for me?

Pause.

Irina   He didn't send for you.

Pause.

Smash cut to flashback, four days earlier, same hut.

Alexei   Thank you for coming.

Irina   What happened? Did you have a fight with them?

Alexei   Yes . . .

Irina   Can it be resolved?

Alexei   Not this time.

She approaches him. Kisses him. **Kate** *'watches'.*

Irina   Come to mine. Stay for a while.

Alexei   You have your life. A job.

Irina   I gave up being a journalist long ago.

She takes out a bottle and they drink.

Irina   What happened?

Alexei   I was dancing with my sister. In the living room. It just struck me.

Pause. He breathes hard.

Alexei   What I had become.

Irina   I don't understand.

Alexei   When I was your age, the world was so big. I drove across Europe, dreamed of America. Freedom. Now I can't even live in my family house.

Pause.

Where do I go? Where do I go, Irina? I don't know.

Irina   It's OK.

Kate *watches.*

Alexei   For so long I thought everyone else was the enemy.
Nikolas, family, politicians, money, officials. But it's me.

He is shaking.

It's in here. I don't know how to be free.

Irina   Come back to mine.

He is shaking.

Irina   Come on.

She touches him. Pause.

Alexei   I don't love you. Never have.

Pause. Silence of the forest. **Kate** *watches.*

Irina   When you came back from Moscow. You flew to
London.

Alexei   That was years ago. Why bring that up?

Pause. She goes to a drawer. Pulls out letters.

Irina   I found these. Her letters to you.

I didn't know you saw her again.

Pause.

Alexei   I didn't. We promised to write while I was on
national service. I never got a single letter. Several years later,
I received a parcel from the Ministry of Defence. They'd
stopped both our letters and kept them in an office in
Novosibursk for seven years.

He gets up, gets the letters.

I went to England to explain to her.

Irina   What happened?

Alexei   I met a man at the front door. A very handsome Englishman. Very charming. With a ring on his finger. End of story.

She holds his hands.

Live your life. You're thirty-one years old, you spend half your life in church, the other half talking to a madman.

Irina   I don't care.

Pause. They are close. Too close. He detaches. Plays the rock'n'roll music again and again. Stop. Start. Stop. Start. Stop.

Alexei   I was thinking. I might go hunting next week.

Irina   You don't hunt.

Alexei   I need some quiet. Drive me out to the forest beyond Tobolsk. I'd just be a few days. Then you could pick me up again.

Irina   I'll come with you.

Alexei   I'd rather be on my own. It'll do me good.

Irina   Do you know your way? It's just trees out there for miles. People get lost.

Pause.

Alexei   I know my way.

Irina   I can take you at the weekend. Come and stay at mine. And then I'll drive you.

They go to the door.

I left my hat.

Alexei *heads out.* **Irina** *comes back in, looks at the letters. Goes to the tape recorder. Plays a few seconds of 'Rip It Up'. Takes out tape. Puts it in one of the envelopes.*

And gives the envelope to **Kate.**

Kate   You sent it.

Scene Twenty-Four

FAILED BBC PRESENTATION

BBC Television Centre. **Michael** *calling* **Kate** *on his phone. Can't get through. 'There is no reception on this mobile phone. There is no reception on this mobile phone.'*

Michael *addresses the BBC people.*

Michael   Hi, thanks for coming. OK, look, we've just cut together the climax to the documentary, partly because it has legal and logistical issues that I'd like someone at the BBC to be addressing over the next few days, and partly because I think it will convince you to broadcast this as soon as schedules allow. All I would say for now is that this has never happened to me in my career before.

He plays the tape to the BBC people. The sound isn't there. **Peter** *has erased it.*

Michael   Can you sort that out, please? That's the wrong sound.

That can't be right.

BBC Sound Guy   That's what we've got, Mr Bellerose.

Michael   No, that's ridiculous. That's clearly not the right sound.

No, just wait, please, where are you going?

Look, don't be stupid. It's clearly not the right sound.

It's not the right sound.

It's not the right sound.

Scene Twenty-Five

FOREST LODGE 2

The forest lodge, 2010. **Kate** *and* **Irina***. A car idling outside.*

Michael *still on stage in London.*

Kate   Where is he?

Irina   In the car. I'm driving him out to Tobolsk today. You know what's beyond there? Nothing.

Michael   It's the wrong sound.

Kate *moves towards the door.* **Irina** *blocks her.*

Tinnitus in **Kate***'s ear.*

Kate   Please just let me go to him.

Irina   Not until you're sure.

Kate   Sure of what?

Irina   Sure you won't leave him again.

Pause.

This life or that one. No in between. No going back. Here or there.

Tinnitus worse. **Michael** *still in the space.*

Irina   I'll give you a minute to decide. Then I drive him out.

Pause. **Kate** *nods.* **Irina** *leaves.* **Kate** *alone.*

Tinnitus worse. Worse.

Michael *stands there.*

Kate *stands there. Noise increasing.*

Alexei *enters.*

Kate *stands between the two men.*

Sudden silence.

Blackout.

UNIVERSITY OF WINCHESTER
LIBRARY

UNIVERSITY OF WINCHESTER
LIBRARY

Afterword: Lost in Russia

Arriving in Russia from the West, it is not unusual to feel that you have walked into a different reality. This impression has little to do with outward appearances. Onion domes apart, Russia isn't exotic in that way. It has to do with the culture of a land which has been shaped by its proximity to the intellectual traditions of Europe.

In Britain, few people are engaged with the idea of freedom. They take it for granted. But Russians, with their history of autocratic governance, are haunted by its seductive promise.

This was never more true than when I started travelling in Russia for my first book, *Epics of Everyday Life*. The year was 1988. A regime which had aspired to impose its vision of the future, to liberate its people from the chains of history and human nature, was entering its death throes.

Gorbachev had recently relaxed the elaborate edifice of state censorship. Every day the revelations of Soviet journalists were chipping away at the ideological monolith. People were consuming newspapers with an insatiable appetite. They were in a collective state of euphoria, obsessed with the idea of freedom. And as a Westerner, a representative of that idea, I was welcomed by strangers wherever I went. The experience was as heady as being in love.

But for the true believers – and there were still many such honest communists – the collapse of their ideology left them badly shaken. 'It's all very well being told to think for ourselves now,' as Andrei admitted to me (I was the first Westerner he had ever met). 'But no one ever taught us how to do that. In our education system there was only ever one answer.'

Back then, Andrei seemed to me like the lost one, lost in his own country. But by the end of 1991, when the Soviet Union was dissolved, the euphoria which had sustained the freedom-seekers had evaporated. I was fighting to keep my own hopes alive when I started my second book, *Lost and Found in Russia*.

In the summer of 1992 I made my way down the River Volga
to the little town of Marx, whose transition from communism
I planned to chronicle. I had chosen it, of all places in Russia,
because it looked as if it would come through the transition
as a prosperous place. It was the main town of a region which
had been newly designated as the homeland for Russia's
Germans, and Germany had promised help and subsidy.

But when I arrived there, instead of a bustle of activity I found
the town falling apart and the townspeople sunk in gloom.
Something had gone wrong with that plan for a homeland for
Russia's Germans. But what? No one would explain. When
I learned that the locals had rebelled against the idea I was
shocked: how could they have sabotaged a plan which would
have transformed their lives? My questions went unanswered.
I came up against a barricade of silence.

This was my first ordeal by silence on my travels. There
would be others. It took more, much more, than charm to
overcome them. For rather than setting out to travel across
the country, I was trying to make my way into the heart of
Russia. So I had to learn what lay behind them. I needed to
become a connoisseur of silences.

In this region which had suffered repeated famines and
collectivisation there was a particular quality of silence when
I asked people about the past. It was a past so toxic that they
could not confront it.

Another silence surrounded the bitter disillusionment with the
West which had succeeded the earlier euphoria. And among
those who had been most in love with that dream of freedom
this silence was most anguished. Once, late at night, my friend
Natasha finally shared with me what that was about: 'We
thought we were different, that when the Party lost power it
would be fine. We thought we'd spend our time being free!
We had no idea how much we'd all become products of
the Soviet system. We knew what we wanted freedom from.
But not what we wanted it for. You in the West were our
dream. And when it collapsed. We blamed you. You weren't
to blame. We just had no idea how to be free. We were like

those prisoners who refuse to leave because they've nowhere else to go. When the Soviet Union fell, the country went through a sort of nervous breakdown. We were looking for a new beginning. We didn't realise that nothing could change until people found themselves.'

Travelling through this scrapyard of hopes and dreams, there were also times when I came to appreciate the importance of these bunkers of silence from a different, more personal, perspective. For now and then I came across things which I did not know how to write about at all. This, for a writer, was not easy. There was the town of gold mines where the workers were seeing collective visions of UFOs and shining beings. I had to tear up draft after draft. I appeared to be mocking those I was writing about. I came across as disbelieving them, when in fact I never doubted the truthfulness of their account, even if I was myself confined to a more conventional reality.

Then there were the experiences which made me feel as if I had walked off the edge of the map of my known world, into territory where my language of Western rationality failed me. For instance, there was a moment when, standing in a reach of virgin forest which stretches half way across Siberia, I heard the forest burst into song. The sky above the trees rang with a sustained chord, the sound of an immense choir, as sonorous as the 'Om' of a cosmic Buddhist meditation. It was glorious – until I realised that I was the only one in our expedition who was hearing this music. What, then, was this music of the spheres? Was it the sound of my own madness? Terrified, I buried that memory in years of silence.

The transition from communism took place against a catastrophic descent into poverty. For Russia's colonies, in taking their independence, had torn the closely interconnected Soviet economy limb from limb. Prices soared: in the first few weeks after the end of communism, they rose by 400 per cent. Inflation took off: within three years it had spiralled by 2,000 per cent. The economy shrank until it was 6 per cent that of the old rival superpower, the United States.

The impact on people's lives was devastating. In Soviet Russia 1.4 per cent had been living on the poverty line; within two years this had risen to 40 per cent. At the end of Soviet power the average age of men was 68. Four years later it had dropped to 58. But I believe that the loss of hope was even more devastating in its effects than the descent into poverty.

I have travelled widely in Russia ever since, chronicling the difficult transition from communism for my book *Lost and Found in Russia*. What continues to fascinate me is how strong the momentum of this idea of freedom remains in people's lives, even when it takes a form unfamiliar to us. As the country has reverted to its autocratic habit of governance, it has swung away from a concept inspired by Europe's tradition towards Russia's Orthodox Church.

We in Europe are inclined to regard this simply as a swing away from the concept of 'freedom'. But many Russians I know would regard this judgement as saying more about us than it does about them. Today, the Western concept of 'freedom' does not bring the crowds out in Russia as it did in Cairo's Tahrir Square. The problem with Western thinking, Russians are apt to remind me, is our inability to understand the idea of spiritual freedom.

Susan Richards is the author of *Lost and Found in Russia* and *Epics of Everyday Life* and founder editor of the online openDemocracy Russia.